ALL ABOUT POO AND WHAT IT CAN DO!

SUPER POOPERS

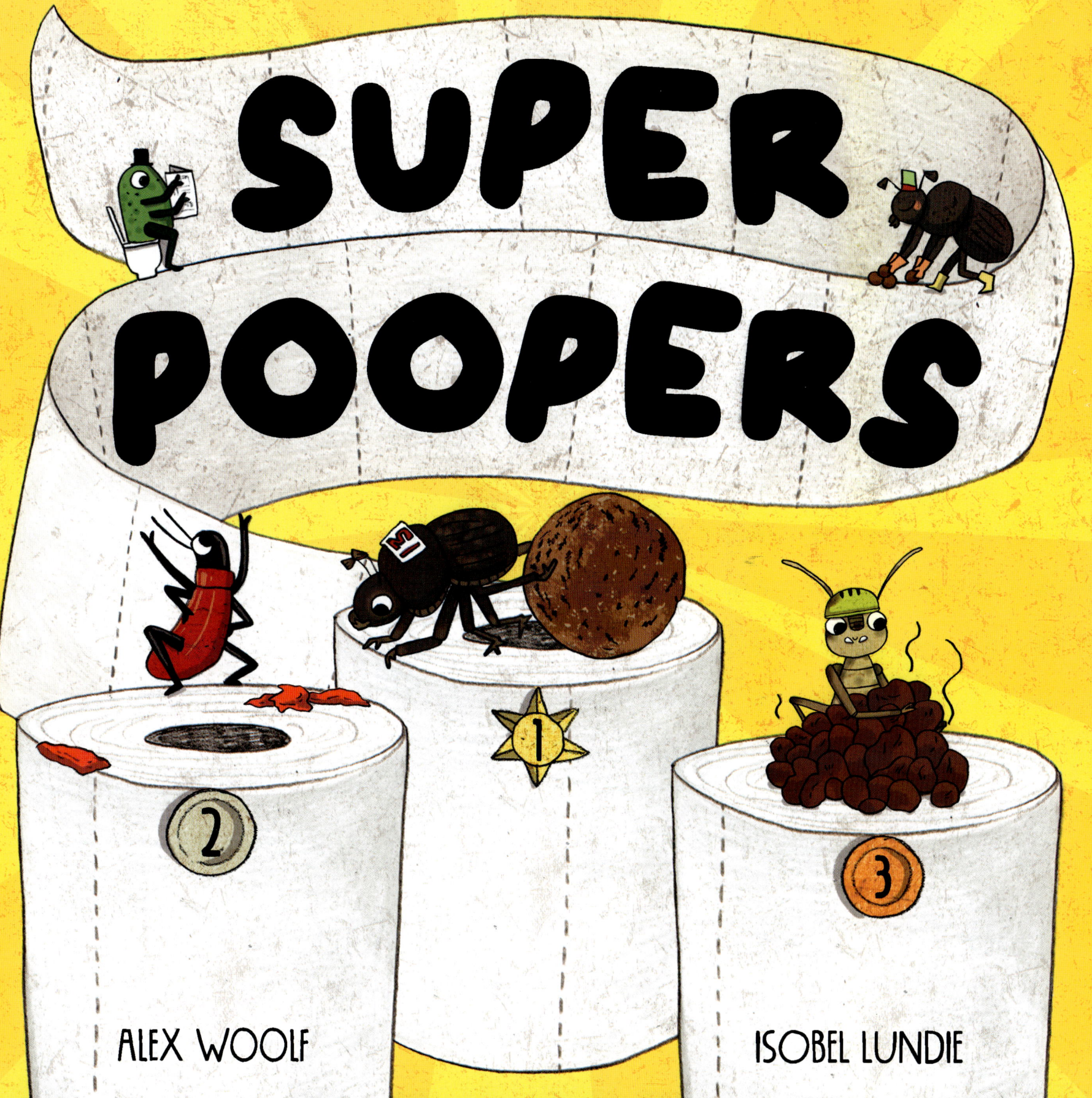

ALEX WOOLF

ISOBEL LUNDIE

Written by
ALEX WOOLF

Illustrated by
ISOBEL LUNDIE

LITTLE TIGER
LONDON

LITTLE TIGER
An imprint of Little Tiger Press Limited
www.littletiger.co.uk
1 Coda Studios, 189 Munster Road, London SW6 6AW
Imported into the EEA by Penguin Random House Ireland,
Morrison Chambers, 32 Nassau Street, Dublin D02 YH68
First published in Great Britain 2023
This edition published 2025
Text by Alex Woolf • Text copyright © Little Tiger Press Limited 2023
Illustrations copyright © Isobel Lundie 2023
A CIP catalogue record for this book is available from the British Library
All rights reserved • ISBN: 978-1-83891-703-6
Printed in China • CPB/2800/2912/1024
10 9 8 7 6 5 4 3 2 1

The Forest Stewardship Council® (FSC®) is a global,
not-for-profit organisation dedicated to the promotion
of responsible forest management worldwide. FSC®
defines standards based on agreed principles for
responsible forest stewardship that are supported by
environmental, social, and economic stakeholders.

To learn more, visit www.fsc.org

CONTENTS

INTRODUCTION

Why do animals poo? Living things need food for energy, growth and health. When the body has digested what it requires, it gets rid of the rest as poo. But nature finds value in everything, even waste. Animals can use poo, or faeces, to mark their territories and communicate. Some eat poo or even live in it.

We humans see poo's potential too. We fertilise crops with it and burn it for heat and power. It's made into face cream, paper and gunpowder. We study it for science, use it in competitions and turn it into art.

In short, there seems to be no end to human and animal ingenuity when it comes to finding uses for poo.

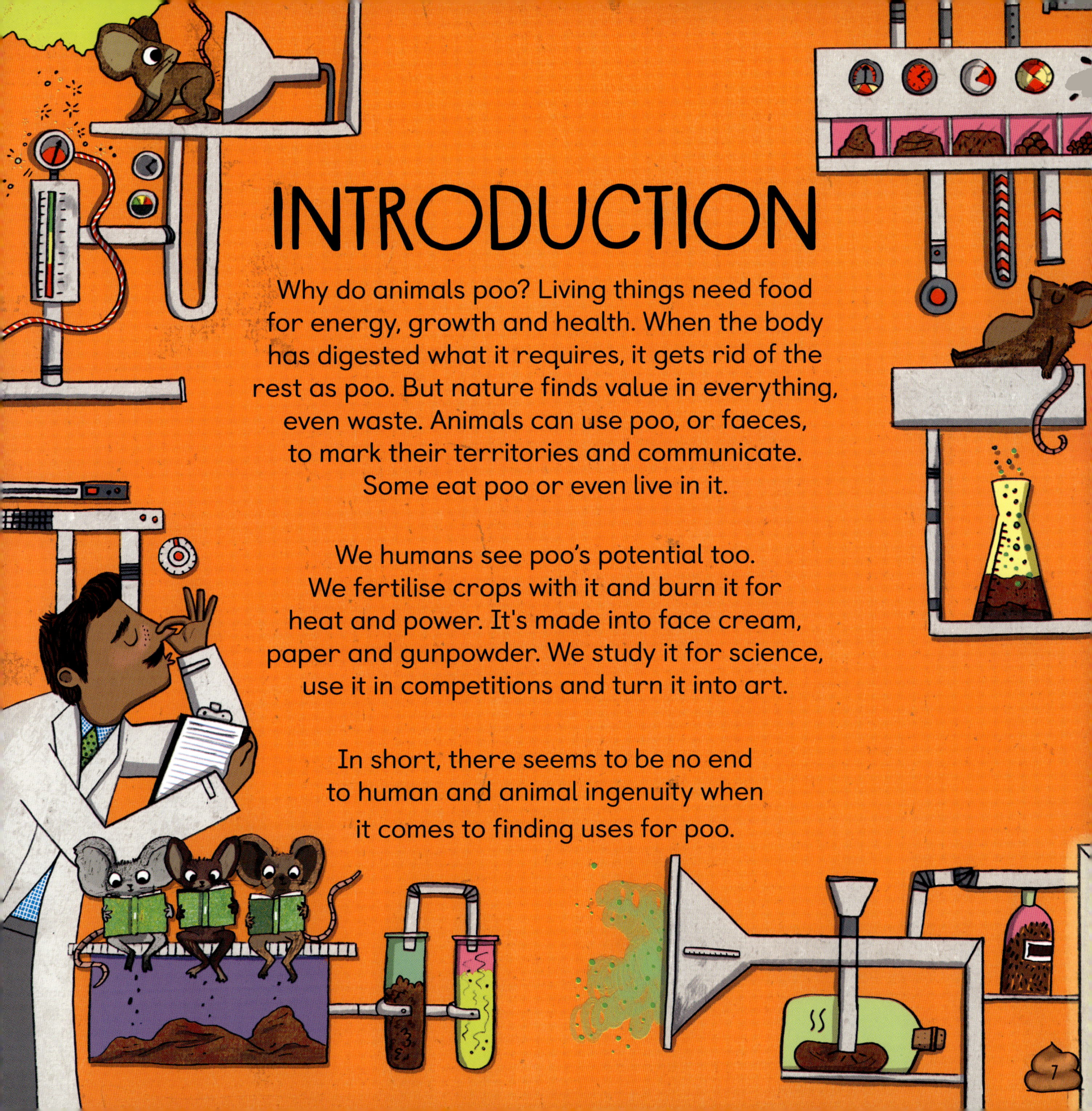

THE CALL OF NATURE

Certain species display fascinating, funny and foul bathroom habits . . .

TREACHEROUS TOILET TRIP

Sloths journey from the treetops to the ground once a week to poo. The trip makes them very vulnerable – more than half of sloth deaths happen during these toilet breaks.

DID YOU KNOW?

A sloth can lose up to a third of its body weight in one poo.

THE POO DANCE

A sloth does a 'poo dance'. It shakes its backside, using its hips and tail to scrape a dung hole and to cover it up afterwards.

It's a hippo-potty-mess!

PLOP SPRAYER

When a hippopotamus poos, it spins its tail, sending dung in all directions. The flying faeces impress the opposite sex and mark territory. Hippo poo spray can reach up to 10m (33ft)!

SHREW LOO

The mountain tree shrew uses the pitcher plant as a toilet. Surprisingly, this benefits them both – the shrew licks nectar while relieving itself and its poo gives the plant nutrients.

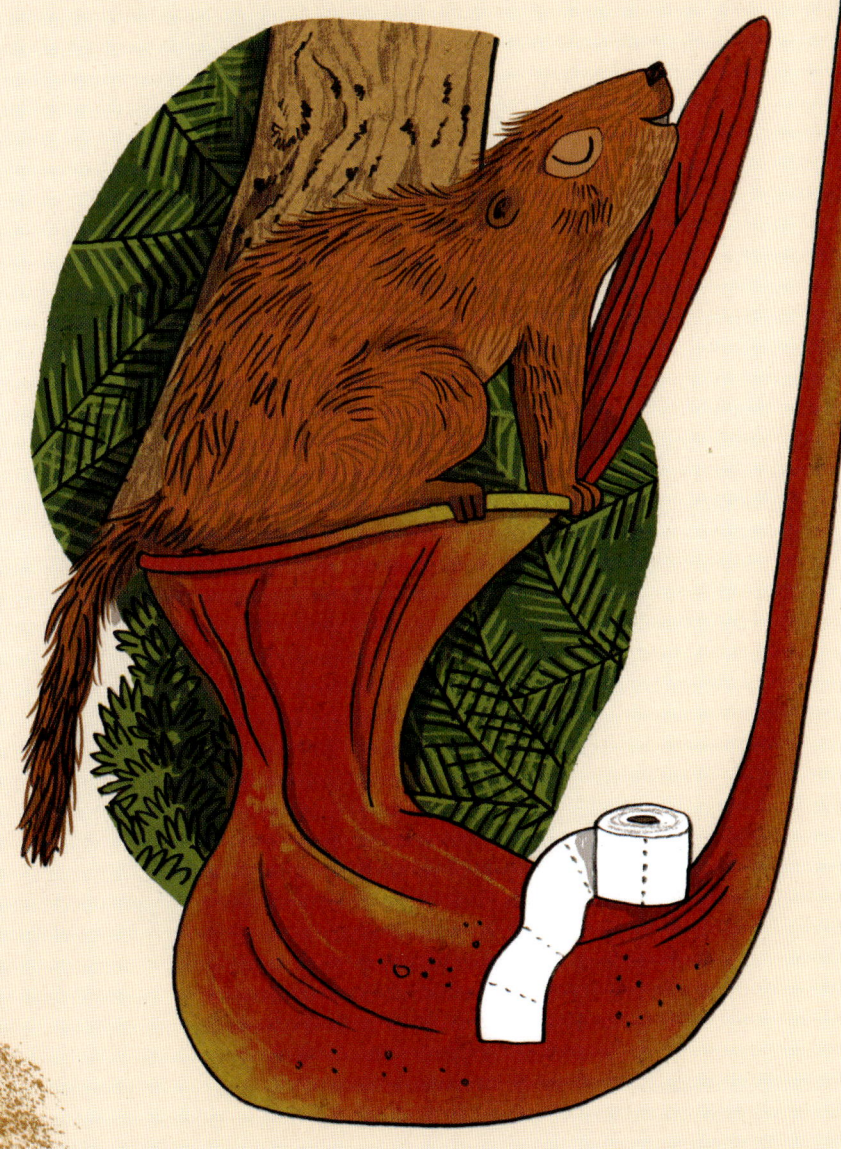

CANINE COMPASS

Dogs can sense the Earth's magnetic field and like to position themselves in a north-south direction when they poop. Nobody knows why.

TOR-POO-DO

Skipper caterpillars fire their frass (poo) up to 40 times their body length. That would be like a human shooting a poo the width of a football pitch! They may do this to keep their homes clean and so that predators can't find them through smell.

MUCKY MARKINGS

Many animals use their wee and poo to say hi to others of their species or to warn them to stay away. This is called scent marking.

DICEY DUNG

The wombat is the only animal with cube-shaped poo. This may be to stop the dung from rolling away so it can be used for marking territory.

LEMUR LATRINES

Numerous creatures have latrines, or shared lavatories, for social networking.

I sensed that we were going to get along!

For example, lemurs sniff their communal toilet trees to know who has been there and whether they would be a good mate. Male lemurs may also poo to warn away intruders.

MIDDEN MESSAGES

Rhinos create big group dung piles, known as middens, which can reach up to 20m (66ft) across. The smell of each rhino's poo gives information about its age, sex, health and suitability as a mate.

Rhinos will often kick their rivals' dung around to make sure that their own poo smells the strongest.

Meet you on a moonlit midden!

This should get me noticed!

REEK AND ROLL

Wolves roll in the urine and faeces of other animals, an activity known as scent rolling. It could be a way of standing out from the crowd or a method of telling other pack members where they've been.

Groups of wolves sometimes roll in the same smelly substances, possibly as a type of pack bonding.

POOPY PALACES

Living in a house made of poo sounds pretty unpleasant,
but for some creatures, dung makes the perfect dwelling place.

TO THE MANURE BORN

What's that smell? The female leaf beetle
is coating her eggs in poo. Gross!

The larvae inside don't seem to mind though.
After they've hatched, they even add to these
coverings with their own faeces . . .

Uh-oh, danger approaching!
But this clever little larva tucks his
head and legs inside his pooey case and
– hey presto! – he looks just like an animal
dropping! What a disgusting disguise!

FURRY FORTIFICATIONS

Some leaf beetle species
plaster the outside of
their casings with the
highly irritating hairs of
the American sycamore
tree. They add attics to
these portable homes
and fill them with more
of the same hairs for
extra protection.

DUNG-ALOW

On the steppes of Central Asia, female black larks use the dung of grazing animals to build their homes. They spend days fetching poo and arranging it carefully around their nests like bizarre patios.

The dung works as a defence because grazing animals don't like trampling on their own droppings. It also insulates the nests from extreme temperatures, keeping them cool in the day and warm at night.

RANK RESIDENCES

There are three main types of dung beetle: tunnellers, dwellers and rollers. Tunnellers burrow beneath poo and drag it into their underground homes. Then they lay eggs in the faeces. When the larvae hatch, they chow down on the poop.

Yummy!

It's our dream home!

SOLD

Dwellers move in to the poo. Their favoured homes tend to be cowpats – the fresher the better. Once they've found somewhere suitable, they spend the rest of their lives there.

I've dung it!

Roller dung beetles are unbelievably strong. One species, the horned dung beetle, can roll poo into a ball up to 1,141 times its own weight, then push it to its burrow. That's the equivalent of a human pushing six full double-decker buses.

14

POO GLUE

Termites are the architects of the insect world. They build giant mounds up to 9m (30ft) tall. The outer walls are made of soil . . .

Let's stick poo-gether!

. . . but the internal chamber walls are constructed from a material called 'carton'. This is made of tiny wood and clay fragments cemented together with poo.

Some termite species build nests inside trees or rotten logs. They use their poo as a plaster to line the nest. They also make the internal walls out of poo.

15

DUNG DEFENCE

For prey animals, life is a never-ending battle for survival. They need a secret weapon against their predators – one option is poo!

Enjoy the hoopoe-roma!

SMELLY SPRAY

The Eurasian hoopoe bird is most vulnerable when newly hatched. To defend itself, the young bird turns around and squirts predators with a stream of liquid faeces.

I hate these poo-poe birds!

DROPPING OUT OF SIGHT

Quick – time for a disguise! This creature is a bird-dung crab spider, so can you guess what she'll pretend to be?

DID YOU KNOW?

As well as looking like poo, bird-dung crab spiders can imitate the dried up splashes of bird droppings with their white silk.

Yes, she's a bird dropping! And what's that smell? She emits a foul stink to drive away predators and attract flies, her main prey!

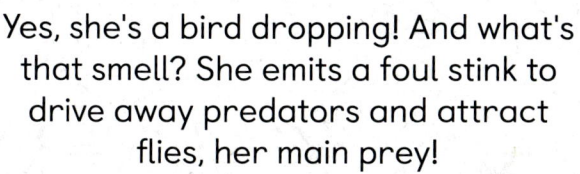

EGG-CELLENT DISGUISE

The African double-banded courser only lays one egg at a time. It does so near antelope poo, which the egg resembles in shape, size and colour. Predators are put off by the risk of ending up with a mouthful of dung!

STINKY FEET

Poo can be used as a defence against overheating too. Vultures defecate on their legs and feet. When the liquid in their faeces evaporates, it cools them down.

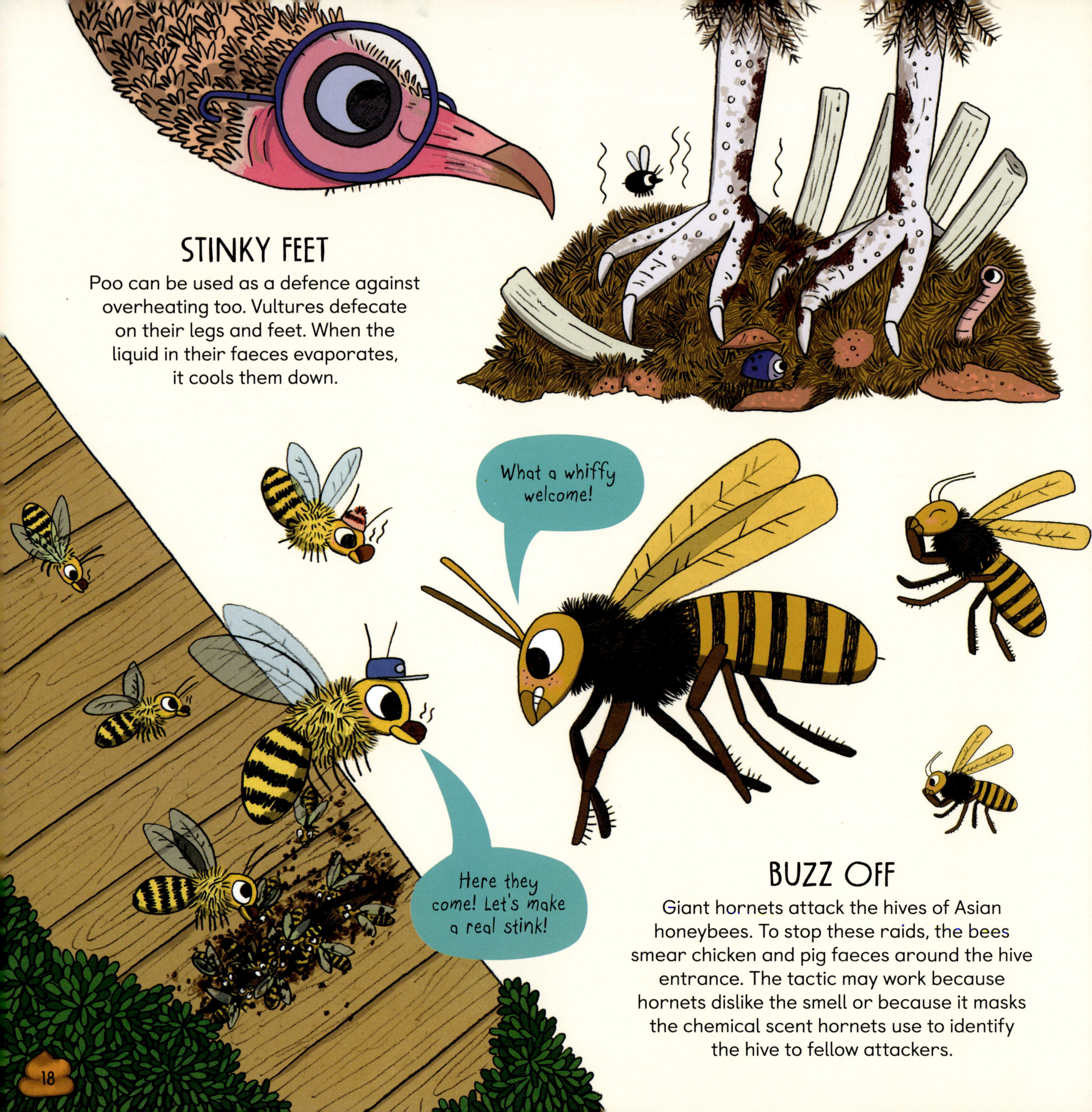

What a whiffy welcome!

Here they come! Let's make a real stink!

BUZZ OFF

Giant hornets attack the hives of Asian honeybees. To stop these raids, the bees smear chicken and pig faeces around the hive entrance. The tactic may work because hornets dislike the smell or because it masks the chemical scent hornets use to identify the hive to fellow attackers.

BOMBS AWAY

A Scandinavian fieldfare spots a raven close to its nest and sounds the alarm.

Launching into action, an attack team showers the threat with poo bombs.

Bullseye! The raven's wings are covered in so much poo it can no longer fly.

IN A SPIN

Sometimes when a sperm whale is disturbed, it will do a poo for protection. It spins its body, creating a massive faecal cloud that cloaks it from view. Then it makes its escape.

19

FEASTING ON FAECES

Eating poo is surprisingly common in the animal kingdom. Faeces contain undigested food, and therefore nutrients, that would otherwise go to waste.

SO GOOD THEY EAT IT TWICE

A rabbit digests softer plant parts in its stomach and small intestine. The tougher bits pass through to the cecum, a pouch at the start of the large intestine.

The cecum partly breaks tough matter down, resulting in a soft, dark poo, known as cecotropes. A rabbit eats its cecotropes to absorb nutrients that it originally missed.

Always recycle! Right, Mum?

DID YOU KNOW?

Other animals that eat their semi-digested poo include hares, pikas, beavers, capybaras and guinea pigs.

CHEW ON THIS

The dung of plant-eaters, or herbivores, contains half-digested grass and a smelly, nutritious liquid. Adult dung beetles feed primarily on the semi-liquid dung. The larvae have the ability to bite and therefore can eat the solid waste.

GUT REACTION

Many baby animals, including elephants and koalas, eat their mothers' droppings. It encourages the growth of healthy bacteria (tiny living things, or organisms) in their guts. This helps their digestion.

Please, take it!

I must prot-ist!

Termites also eat each other's poo to build up communities of tiny organisms called protists in their guts. Without protists, they wouldn't be able to digest tough plant fibre.

FRUIT POOP

The poo of the Australian cassowary contains lots of half-digested fruit that still has plenty of nutrition. The birds therefore eat each other's droppings, as well as their own.

MOTHERLY MOLE-RATS

In a naked mole-rat colony, one queen produces all the babies, while other females are infertile. But they eat her poo, which has high levels of a natural substance called oestrogen. This prompts them to feed and care for the queen's many babies.

VAIN VULTURES

The Egyptian vulture feeds on cow, sheep and goat droppings because they contain substances called carotenoids. Carotenoids are nutritious and also turn the vulture's face yellow, making it more attractive to potential mates.

POO AND THE PLANET

Animal poo is world-changing. It can create beaches, strengthen coral reefs and spread plant seeds.

THE WHALE TRAIL

Whales dive deep in search of food. When they return from the depths, they do a big poo.

This dung moves nutrients from the deep ocean up to the surface. The process is known as the 'whale pump'.

I have to thank that whale!

The nutrients in the whale faeces encourage the growth of minuscule living things called phytoplankton.

These are eaten by fish.

Fish are eaten by larger marine predators and seabirds.

These in turn may feed land mammals. Whale poo brings deep ocean nutrients onto land.

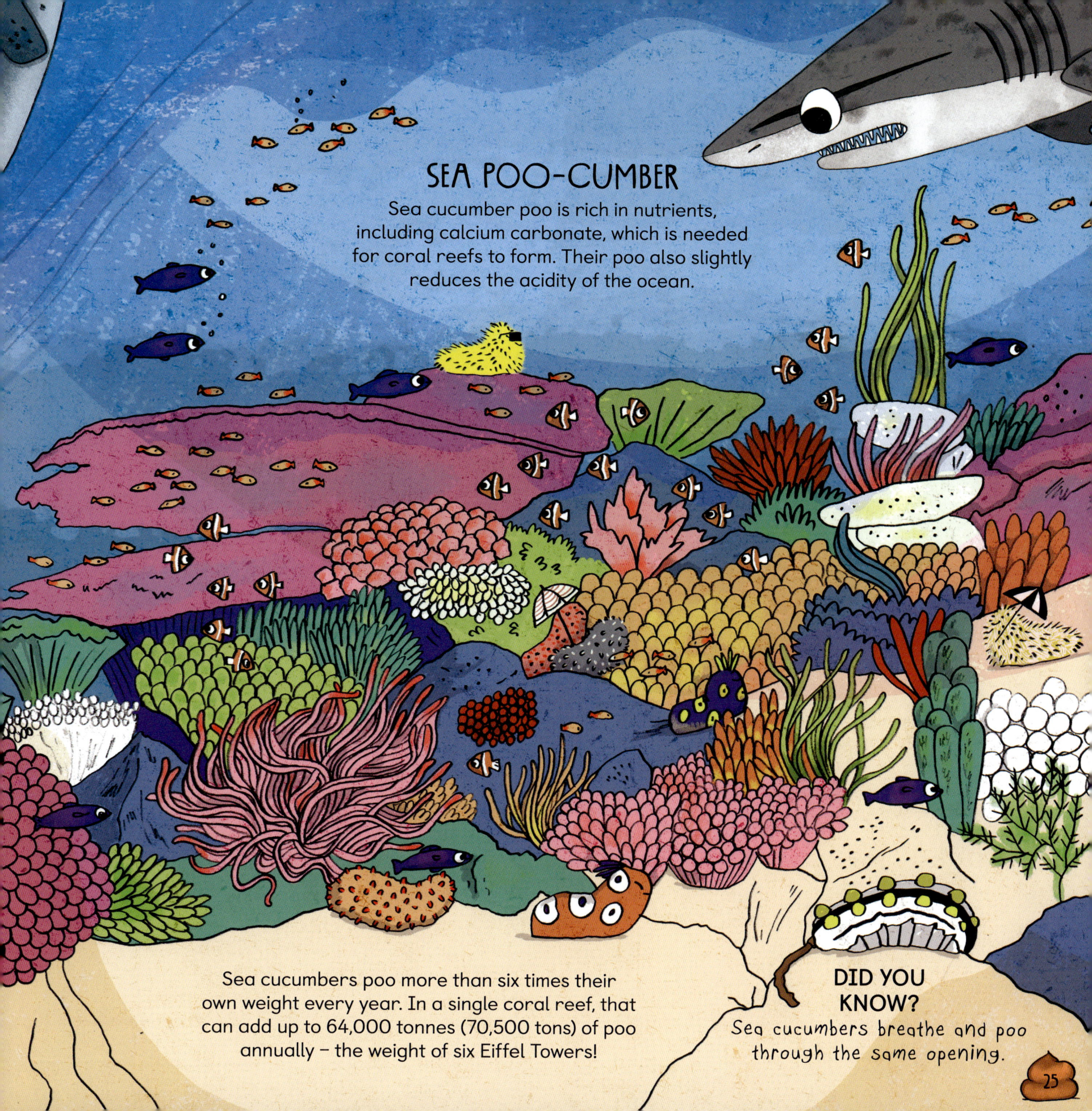

SEA POO-CUMBER

Sea cucumber poo is rich in nutrients, including calcium carbonate, which is needed for coral reefs to form. Their poo also slightly reduces the acidity of the ocean.

Sea cucumbers poo more than six times their own weight every year. In a single coral reef, that can add up to 64,000 tonnes (70,500 tons) of poo annually – the weight of six Eiffel Towers!

DID YOU KNOW?

Sea cucumbers breathe and poo through the same opening.

25

PLANT EX-POO-DITION

Mmm, delicious! This bird has spotted some tasty berries. Plants encase their seeds in fruit so that animals will eat them and move the seeds somewhere new.

The little seed is tough. It has a strong coating to survive digestion. Some seeds even have to pass through two digestive systems if the animal that ate the seed is eaten in turn . . .

Better duck if you don't want a turd's eye view! The seed is being pooped out somewhere else.

A new plant is growing!
Both plant and bird have done their business.

DUNES OF DUNG

The beautiful white sand on tropical beaches is actually parrotfish poo! Parrotfish are small, beaked fish that live around coral reefs. They bite off bits of the reef and grind it up before pooing out sand.

Thank you, parrotfish!

The average parrotfish poops around 100kg (220lb) of sand a year. That's about the same weight as a giant panda!

This can be good for coral reefs because the parts the parrotfish eats are often diseased. The parrotfish also leaves a surface on which new coral can grow.

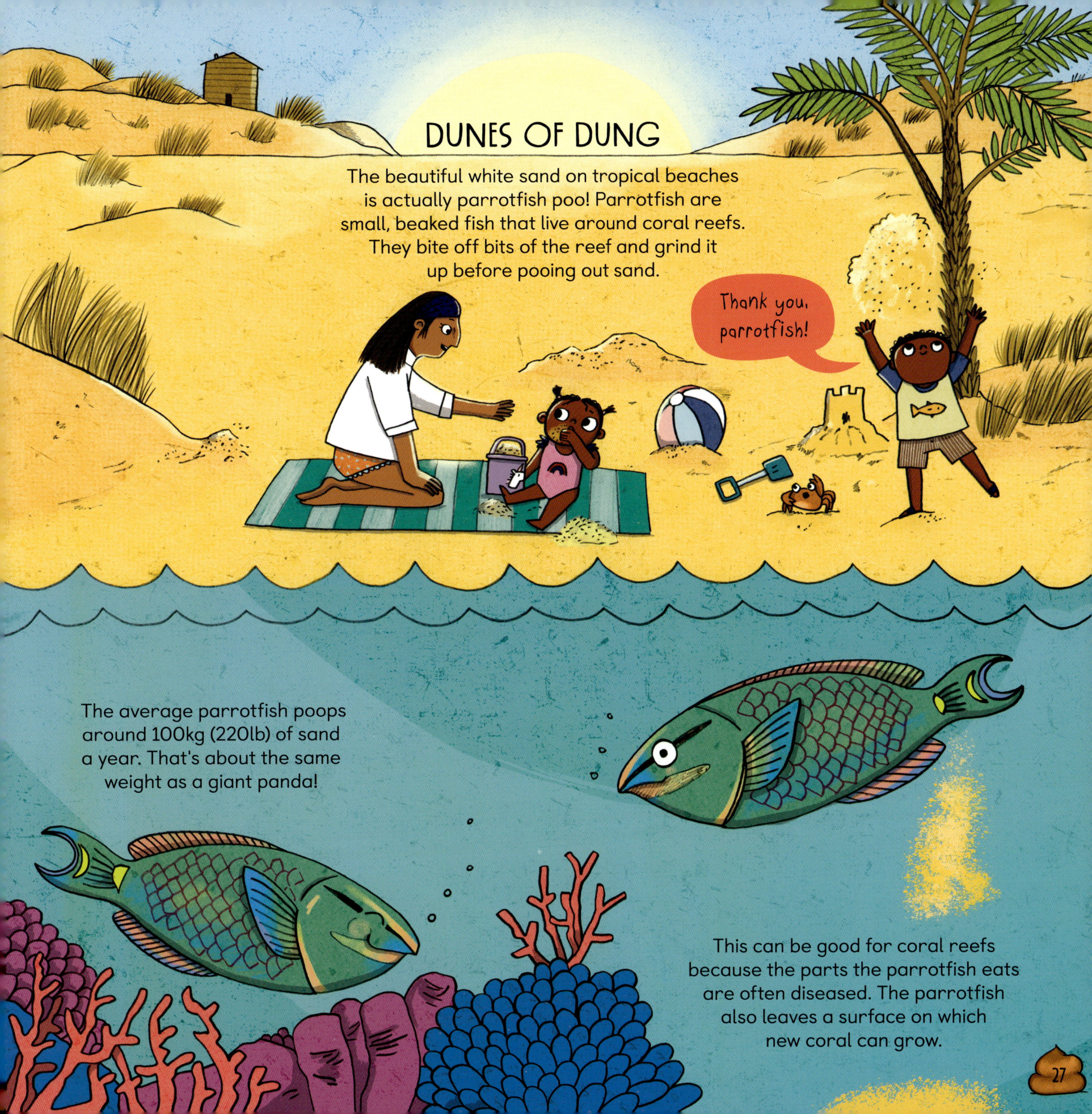

POWER FROM POO

It's strange to think, but our bodies constantly manufacture a substance that could provide light and heat for our homes and fuel for our vehicles: poo!

FROM FAECES TO FUEL

To get power from poo, it first needs to be placed in an airless vessel called an anaerobic digester. The vessel is warmed, causing the bacteria inside it to turn the poo into a biogas, which can be burned to generate heat and power.

Every little bit helps!

DRIVEN BY DUNG

Humans have been burning animal dung for cooking and heating for thousands of years. We still use poo for energy today. In Grand Junction in Colorado, USA, human waste is turned into fuel for a fleet of 40 public service vehicles, including street sweepers and buses.

WARMTH FROM WASTE

In Nakuru County, Kenya, a company manufactures blocks of fuel made out of human faeces for cooking and heating. The waste is dried and treated to remove dangerous bacteria. The blocks are odourless and burn well for a long time.

POOCH POO LIGHTING

Dogs produces almost 3,000 tonnes (3,300 tons) of waste each day in the UK. One solution to this plethora of poo is to turn it into light. In the Malvern Hills in England, inventor Brian Harper has created a street lamp powered by canine poo donated by passing dog walkers.

FABULOUS FERTILISER

Poo helps to make plants grow. Farmers have been fertilising their crops with animal dung, or manure, for at least 8,000 years. Don't let that put you off your food!

This soil is poo-tiful!

It really is re-muck-able!

MARVELLOUS MANURE

Manure adds important nutrients to the soil which help plants grow. It loosens soil so it can absorb and store water. It also reduces run-off – the removal of nutrients from soil when it rains.

Fresh manure has high levels of a nutrient called nitrogen. It is vital for plant growth but can also dry plants out. Over time, the nitrogen and other substances in the manure become less harmful, so manure is composted, or left to settle, for several months. The manure also becomes less smelly – good news for gardeners!

BIRD POO BATTLES

On the islands off Peru, there are massive piles of bird poo, or guano, up to 46m (150ft) high. The guano is an excellent fertiliser and numerous countries started mining it in the mid-19th century. In 1879, Peru and Bolivia even went to war with Chile, partly over control of the guano.

PANDA POO TEA

The world's most expensive tea costs around £140 a cup. The secret of its unique flavour? Panda poo fertiliser. Pandas eat nothing but wild bamboo and digest only around 30% of the nutrients. The rest goes into their dung.

DID YOU KNOW?
Pandas poop around 40 times a day, so there'll be no fertiliser shortage!

MADE FROM MUCK

Poo is used around the world to make all sorts of unexpected things, including homes, paper, gunpowder and coffee.

DUNG DWELLINGS

Cob is one of the earliest building materials. It is made from soil, clay, straw and cow dung. In many countries, cow dung is still used to make bricks and plaster. It dries hard like cement, emits no smell, keeps the heat in and repels insects.

Dung! Those are fine bricks!

Do you pay-per poo?

POO PAPER

In Thailand, a company called Poo Poo Paper makes paper from elephant poo. The poo is rinsed and boiled to disinfect it and remove the smell. The resulting pulp is mixed with plant fibres, then spread on mesh trays and baked under the Sun into paper.

DID YOU KNOW?
A single elephant can produce up to 100kg (220lb) of dung a day — enough for 115 sheets of paper.

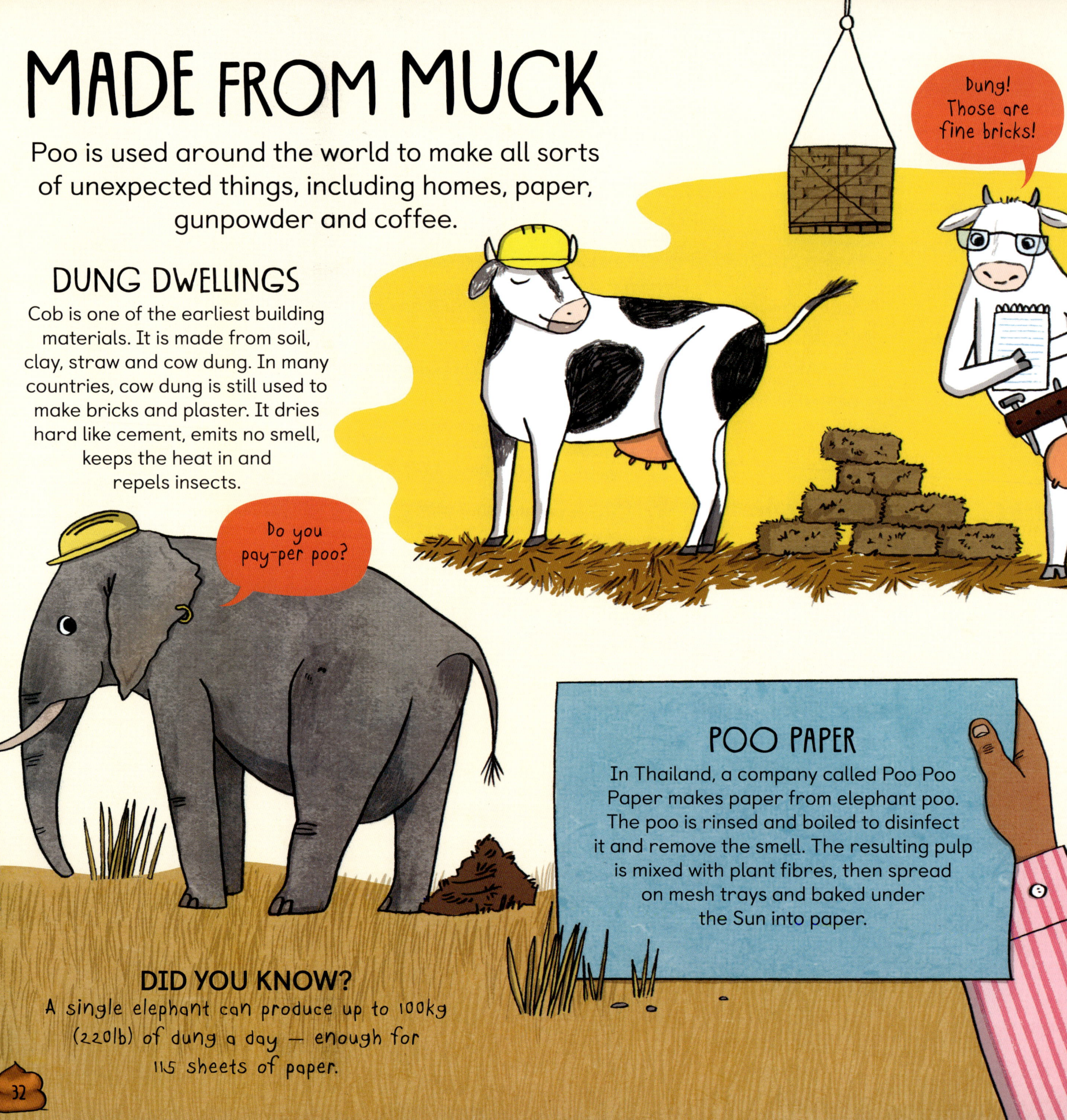

WAX FROM WASTE

Shellac is a shiny, waxy glaze used in a range of things from sweets and fruit wax to nail varnish and chairs. It is secreted by an insect called the lac bug and is found on trees in the forests of India and Thailand.

Shellac is filtered to remove insect parts and wood shavings before it is added to products. But you may still think twice next time you bite into a shiny sweet!

I've taken a shine to you!

SHAMPOO

15 MINUTES

HAIR

Jelly Beans

NAIL VARNISH

Nailz

NAIL

CUP-A-POOP

Kopi luwak is a luxury coffee made from beans collected from Asian palm civet poo. The drink is particularly smooth because the civet's digestive juices break down the parts of the bean that make coffee bitter.

Indonesian plantation workers in the 19th century first tried civet poo coffee because they weren't allowed to pick coffee beans for their own use under the Dutch colonial regime. Today, it sells for up to £70 a cup!

Dropping in for a cuppa?

OFFER £69.99!

DID YOU KNOW?

There is a Chinese tea made from the droppings of grain moth larvae that chomp on tea leaves.

GUAN-POWDER

Bat droppings are full of saltpetre, a key ingredient of gunpowder. During the American Civil War (1861–65), the South began large-scale harvesting of this guano for explosives after the North blocked off supplies from the seaports.

I've goat to poop!

BEAUTY AND THE BEAST

Argan oil is a luxury oil used in beauty products and produced from the nuts of the argan tree. In Morocco, goats clamber up these trees 8–10m (26–33ft) high to munch on the fruits. They bring the nuts to the ground for the farmers to harvest, though there is some debate about whether the nuts are pooped out undigested or the goats spit them out. Nowadays, mechanical harvesting is often used, but goats can still be seen dining in the trees.

SNIFFING FOR SCAT

How can we learn more about wild animals? Some clues are in their poo! Animal poo, or scat, can tell us a lot about a creature's lifestyle, habits and migration patterns.

DETECTING DIET IN DUNG

Researchers analyse scat samples to learn about an animal's diet. A herbivore's poo may be full of seeds, showing what fruit and berries it's eating. A carnivore's may contain bones and fur, giving an indication of its prey.

I'm feeling a little low.

SIGNS OF STRESS IN STOOLS

By studying scat, scientists can learn about an animal's reproductive cycle and if it is suffering from stress. Researchers examining the poo of clouded leopards in zoos discovered the animals became stressed when they weren't given enough hiding nooks or tall places to climb.

36

GENETIC POO PRINT

Animal scat contains DNA – molecules inside the animal's cells that carry the instructions it needs to live, grow and reproduce. From the DNA, researchers can estimate population size of an animal group, gender ratios and the relationships between the group's members. This is useful information for discovering more about the lives of endangered species.

Scientists studied the DNA in the scat of the highly endangered northern muriqui monkey of Brazil. They learned that young males were much more likely to find mates if they remained close to their mothers.

You'll make a prime mate!

MUM

ANCIENT EXCREMENT

Poo can tell us lots about the past. Fossilised faeces, known as coprolites, give us hints about ancient animals' diets, health and migrations.

MEAT ON THE MENU

Hadrosaurs were thought to be herbivores until scientists in Montana and Utah, USA, discovered the remains of snail shells and crustaceans in their coprolites.

DID YOU KNOW?

Scientists have found coprolites dating back to as far as 480 million years ago. Talk about the origin of faeces!

PRIMAEVAL PASTURE

Scientists have learned that dinosaurs living 65 million years ago dined on grass. This was unexpected because it was previously believed that grass didn't exist at that time.

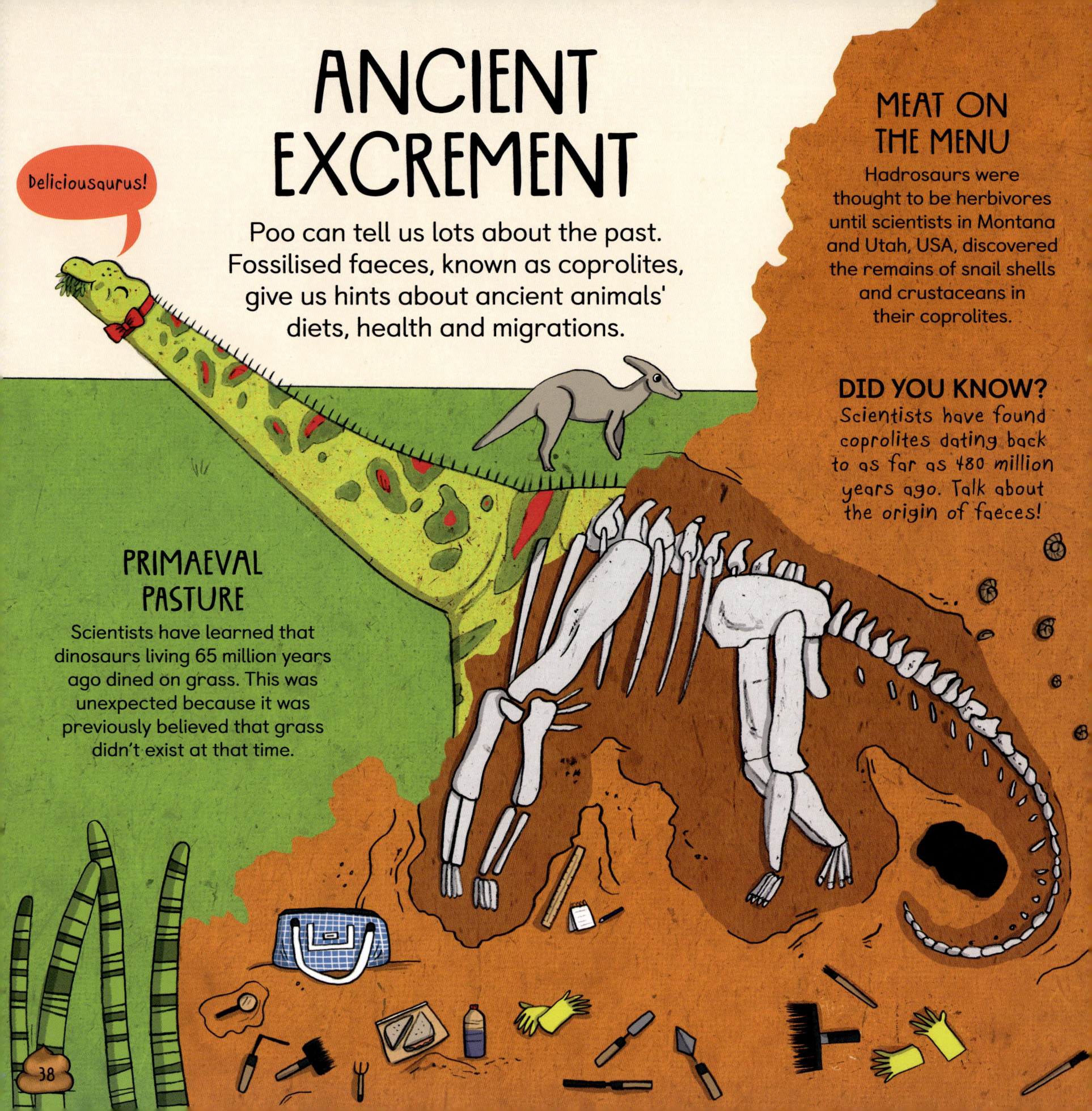

You might not want to walk there!

How much further? I'm all pooped out!

HISTORY FROM HORSE DUNG

GAUL | ITALY

One of ancient history's most epic journeys was the crossing of the Alps by the Carthaginian general Hannibal and his army (complete with elephants!) during one of their wars against Rome (218–201 BC).

Archaeologists took soil samples from the mountain pass through which Hannibal was thought to have crossed from France into Italy. They found it was rich in horse manure dating from around 200 BC. The dung may be physical evidence of this legendary journey.

39

THE TURD TIMES

PECULIAR USES OF POO

Throughout history, humans have found some odd and eccentric uses for poo. Get the scoop here.

HELP WANTED *pure finder*

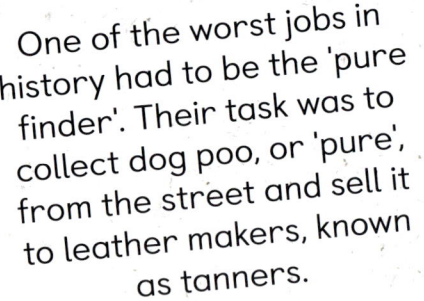

★ SMELL FOR LEATHER ★

One of the worst jobs in history had to be the 'pure finder'. Their task was to collect dog poo, or 'pure', from the street and sell it to leather makers, known as tanners.

Dog poo was first used in leather-making in the second half of the 18th century because it was good for cleansing and softening tough leather fibres. It also gave the final leather product a beautiful sheen. By the mid-20th century, industrially produced chemicals were used instead.

BIZARRE BINGO

In cow pie bingo, chalk squares are drawn and numbered on an enclosed, grassy field. Players pay for a square. When all the squares have been sold, a cow is released into the field to graze.

BIZARRE BINGO

The players wait with bated breath to see where it will do its business. The owner of the square that receives the first 'cow pie' wins the game.

She must have great smelling skin!

A beauty treatment in Japan involves smearing nightingale guano on your face. Known as *uguisu no fun*, the facial was first used in the 17th century by Kabuki (dance-drama) performers to repair skin damage caused by heavy make-up.

The droppings contain a substance called guanine that lightens dark circles and blemishes, and urea (a product found in urine), which keeps skin moist.

EXCREMENTAL ART

I love food art!

In the 1990s, British artist Chris Ofili created a series of paintings using elephant dung. He was inspired by the small, round elephant droppings he saw during a visit to Zimbabwe.

DID YOU KNOW?
In 2013, a San Francisco gallery hosted an art show of paintings made from animal faeces.

FLUNG DUNG

Cow-chip throwing is a popular sport in Beaver, Oklahoma, USA. Players fling cow chips – dried discs of cow dung – either like a Frisbee or ball as far as they can.

A similar contest takes place in the rural town of Krylovo in central Russia. Cow-dung flinging also occurs in the village of Kairuppala in southern India. Here, locals split into two groups and hurl the cowpats at each other as part of a religious ceremony to celebrate a marriage dispute between two deities.

POO-RIOUSER AND POO-RIOUSER

You can't go just yet. Discover some terrific turd trivia in the five faecal facts below!

Arguably, the blue whale creates the largest poos in nature. It can excrete 200 litres at a time.

If you laid out all the toilet rolls used in China in one year, it would be six and a half billion km (four billion miles) long, which is further than the distance from Earth to Neptune.

The Demodex mite is a microscopic parasite that lives on people's eyelids. It eats but has no anus, making it one of the very few creatures that doesn't poo. Instead, it just stores waste in its body for the whole of its two-week lifespan.

The six Apollo missions have left 96 bags of waste on the Moon in total. If any of the microbes on the poo have survived, this could have important implications for helping life endure in outer space, especially on Mars.

The jellyfish only has a single hole through which it both eats and excretes.